What are human rights?

Legal rights

A **right** is something to which everyone is entitled. Legal rights come from the law. For example, people have the legal right to vote in the United Kingdom once they are 18 years old.

The origins of legal rights can be found in ancient history. In Athens in ancient Greece, the right to vote was given to all citizens. This included local men, but not women, children, slaves or foreign...

Moral right...

The United Nations is a group...
moral rights, which can be a...
aimed to create a political sys...
constitution of France, a decla...
the moral rights of French citi...

The Univer... Declaratio... Human Rig...

Modern **human rights** were defin...
World War II. People in many coun...
with the atrocities that had occurre...
resolved that these atrocities would...

In response to this, the **Univer...**
Human Rights (or UDHR) was si...
1948. Representatives of the 48 co...
Nations in 1948 signed the docume...
Declaration was designed as a safe...
human rights of people around the...

The first section states, "all hu...
free and equal in dignity and rights...
with reason and conscience, and sh...
one another in a spirit of brotherho...
that the Universal Declaration takes...
recommends that human beings tre...
Unfortunately, however, human righ...
occurring across the world today.

Universal rights

The Universal Declaration's name suggests that rights should be universal – they should apply to everyone everywhere. Article 2 of the Declaration states that "Everyone is entitled to all the rights and freedoms set forth in this Declaration, without distinction of any kind." This means that the Universal Declaration is meant to be applied to every person belonging to every country in the world today.

What the Declaration contains

The Universal Declaration of ... n Rights contains 30 specific ...ns of text. These sections are ... as articles. When a country ...s a specific human right in a ...ular article, they are said to ... violated an article of the ...sal Declaration".

...rbia, where there were wide scale

Why do you think Article 2, which aims to include everyone in the world, was included in the Universal Declaration of Human Rights?

A variety of different rights

How the Declaration works in practice

Once the United Nations passed the Universal Declaration of Human Rights, a **UN Commission on Human Rights** was set up. The role of the Commission is threefold:

- monitoring countries for signs of human rights abuses, such as cases of **torture**, use of the death penalty, and sexual or racial **discrimination**
- once the Commission has evidence of **human rights** abuses, it collects information. This is then reported to representatives of the United Nations.
- finally, the Commission liaises with governments and other interested groups to improve human rights in countries across the world.

Often, the UN Commission on Human Rights is assisted by non-governmental organizations (NGOs). One example of an NGO is the charity **Amnesty International**, which monitors human rights abuses worldwide and campaigns against them. Amnesty International has over 10 million members worldwide.

Has the Declaration been a success?

For the 50 years it has been in operation, the Universal Declaration of Human Rights has had mixed success. Undoubtedly it has made a difference in many different countries, at one time or another. Political prisoners have been released in many countries – such as Chile, Indonesia and the USSR – because **pressure groups** were able to highlight breaches of the Universal Declaration of Human Rights.

However, many human rights abuses still take place around the world. For example, the death penalty still exists in many countries, including the USA (see page 29). Also, political unrest has led to human rights abuses in parts of the former Yugoslavia, as has the continuation of the one party state in China. Here, freedom of expression is restricted.

The right to freedom of peaceful assembly and association is set out in Article 20 of the Universal Declaration. This photograph shows a student confronting army tanks near Tiananmen Square, Beijing. In June 1989, over 1000 people were killed when the Chinese army was sent to break up a peaceful pro-democracy protest attended by thousands of students and other ordinary people. This was widely condemned as an abuse of human rights.

A declaration or a convention?

The Universal Declaration for Human Rights is not legally binding. In other words, it does not make up part of the law of the member states of the UN. Instead, it is merely a set of rights that countries have agreed to work towards. This means that a person cannot be taken to court for breaching the Universal Declaration of Human Rights.

In order to provide a legal basis for human rights, some European countries decided to create the **European Convention on Human Rights** (see page 3). The Convention is legally binding. In other words, when someone breaks the Convention, they can be taken to court.

Previously, human rights groups have argued that the Universal Declaration should be made law. Cases of human rights abuses could then be brought before the World Court (see page 28).

However, governments have resisted this so far. They argue that they would lose too much power, or national sovereignty. Governments add that it is more democratic for local citizens, representatives and judges to decide how to interpret human rights in their own country, rather than have rights imposed by the United Nations.

Discuss

"In the 21st century, it is time that the Universal Declaration of Human Rights was made a convention, so that it is legally binding on member countries." Do you agree? Give reasons for your views.

Human rights in Europe

In order to provide human rights with a legal framework, the European Convention on Human Rights was passed in 1963, by all the members of the Council of Europe. Today, the council contains 44 members, who wish to uphold human rights. The Council of Europe is not the same thing as the European Union. However, the 15 EU member states are all members of the Council of Europe.

The European Court of Human Rights

When someone breaks the European Convention on Human Rights, they can be brought to court. In order to take a case to the European Court of Human Rights in Strasbourg, an individual must first have the case heard in their own country.

Before the introduction of the UK Human Rights Act (see below), individuals had to bring long and complex cases through the British legal system, before they could take them to Europe. Nevertheless, on more than 50 occasions, the European Court of Human Rights disagreed with the British courts.

The UK Human Rights Act

In order to make the system simpler, the Government decided to incorporate the European Convention on Human Rights into UK law in 1998. This means that a UK judge can now consider the European Convention in a UK court. It also means that everyone – schools, hospitals, small businesses – must consider the human rights in the European Convention before they make decisions.

Rights as freedoms

A wide variety of rights were included in the Universal Declaration. Some of these rights are called freedoms. These include:

● Article 4: freedom from slavery
● Article 19: freedom to express an opinion
● Article 20: freedom of peaceful assembly.

It is these rights that the European Convention on Human Rights mirrors.

Rights as entitlements

However, other rights exist. Some political commentators call these rights **entitlements**, rather than natural rights. These include:

● Article 17: the right to property
● Article 24: the right to rest and leisure
● Article 26: the right to an education.

These rights are not included in the European Convention.

The European Charter of Fundamental Rights

In 1998, the European Union decided it wanted to expand the rights of people in its member states. The European Parliament, the European Commission, and the 15 European Governments agreed on the European Charter of Fundamental Rights.

This contains 50 new articles of human rights, including many freedoms and entitlements in both the Universal Declaration and the European Convention. Some of the new rights were to take account of new technology (see page 30). Other new rights include:

● the right to limits on working hours, and annual paid holiday
● the right to consumer protection, to ensure consumer safety.

In 2002, the 15 member states had not agreed how the Charter of Fundamental Rights was to be enforced. As a result, there are no laws or a court to enforce these rights yet.

The European Commission of Human Rights

When the European Convention on Human Rights was passed, the **European Commission of Human Rights** was set up. This includes judges from each member state of the Council of Europe in the European Union.

The job of the Commission is to see that human rights are upheld in all the countries of the European Union. If any individual, group, or non-governmental organization (for example, a pressure group or charity) feels its human rights have been violated, it can write to the Commission. The Commission can then decide whether to pass the case on to the European Court of Human Rights.

Discuss

Look at 'Rights as freedoms' and 'Rights as entitlements'. Which rights do you think are the most important? Why?

Children's rights

Vulnerable

One group of people who have had their rights consistently violated are children. Without parents and sympathetic adults to protect them, children become the most vulnerable group of people in any sort of society.

UNICEF

In 1946, the United Nations created UNICEF – the United Nations International Children's Emergency Fund. UNICEF exists to protect the rights of children and it works closely with governments, pressure groups and charities such as the NSPCC (the National Society for the Prevention of Cruelty to Children) and Anti-Slavery International.

The UN became so concerned about children's rights being abused that in 1959 it passed the Declaration of the Rights of the Child. This formed the basis for the **United Nations Convention on the Rights of the Child**.

The United Nations Convention on the Rights of the Child (UNCRC)

The United Nations Convention on the Rights of the Child specifically states the rights of children. Like the Universal Declaration of Human Rights (see pages I and 2), the UNCRC is international. This means that the rights are universal and should be upheld in all countries. Unlike the Declaration, it is a Convention, which means that it has legal authority. In other words, it is illegal to break the Convention in the countries which have signed it.

In order for the Convention to become international law, 20 countries had to sign it. The United Kingdom signed in April 1990 and the Convention became law in January 1992.

All children have the right to happiness

Survival rights

This includes the right to health and a decent standard of living. Of particular importance is the right to food and clean water.

Development rights

This includes the right to a free and full education for children of all ages. There is also the right to information, so children have the knowledge they need to make decisions about their own lives.

In addition, the right to freedom of thought, conscience and religion is mentioned here. Most importantly, the right to play – a special right for children – is included.

Protection rights

Protection rights are included to protect those rights set out above. However, the Convention also includes protection against slavery, exploitation, cruelty and enforced separation from a family. The latter means that it is against the Convention for a person, company or other organization to split up a child from his or her parents, against the child's will.

Participation rights

This allows children the freedom to express an opinion on any issue that affects them, including their health care and education.

How it works

In order to make the Convention work, the United Nations set up a special committee of ten experts to oversee it. The committee monitors countries for signs that children's rights are being abused. For example, are there a large number of young children working in one country?

The United Nations also supplies technical support and assistance. This can include trainers to provide more teachers, qualified nurses to provide health education, and lawyers to work on improving laws to protect children in a particular country. The committee also contacts other agencies to see how they can help.

What needs to be done in the UK

The United Nations Convention on the Rights of the Child has been ratified in the UK. This means that Parliament has passed laws to protect the rights of children in the UK.

In addition to this, the Welsh Assembly and Scottish Parliament have created a Children's Commissioner to protect children's rights in Wales and Scotland. Northern Ireland seems set to follow this move. In early 2002, pressure groups were campaigning for a Children's Commissioner for human rights in England.

The job of the English Commissioner would be to investigate cases where children's rights may be being abused. The Commissioner would also coordinate a strategy to improve children's rights in England.

Discuss

1 The United Nations Convention on the Rights of the Child mentions the right to play. Do you think all children should be entitled to the right to play? Give reasons.

2 Imagine you were invited to a discussion group to talk about children's rights issues. What issues would you raise?

The right to an education

Article 25 of the UDHR states that "Everyone has the right to an education. Education shall be free, at least at primary and secondary school. Primary school education shall be compulsory. Higher education shall be equally accessible to all on the basis of merit."

Despite this, the right to an education is one of the most widely abused of human rights across the world today. At the end of the 20th century, there were at least 1.5 billion people who were illiterate – they could not read or write.

The situation seems to be getting worse. For example, in Southeast Asia, the number of illiterate people is set to double in the next 30 years. Here, 50 per cent of adults do not know how to read and 75 per cent of adults did not have the chance to even complete primary school.

Two main reasons exist which prevent children across the world from fulfilling their right to an education – war and conflict, and a lack of money.

War and conflict

Since World War II, there have been over 190 wars and many civil conflicts across the world. These have had a devastating effect on children's education, as schools are destroyed, and children are either abused or exploited as child soldiers.

In the last 10 years, 35 countries have used child soldiers in conflicts, with appalling effects. Children as young as six have been forced to join armies. UNICEF estimates that 2500 boy soldiers died in one single battle during the Iran-Iraq war in the 1980s.

These child soldiers march through Goma before being sent to various posts as active fighters for the Democratic Alliance for the Liberation of Congo Zaire

Discuss

1   Read 'After the war in Sierra Leone'. Imagine you had only morning lessons and the materials available at Koya in Sierra Leone. Which subjects would you concentrate on? Why?

2   "Primary education for everyone is the most important human right, and governments should make it their top priority." Do you agree? Or are there other human rights you consider more important? Why?

Education – a cash crisis

In southern Africa, education is starved of resources. Sub-Saharan Africa receives less than 10 per cent of the World Bank's education lending. This figure has been dropping now for a number of years.

Despite this, UNICEF has calculated that education for all would cost less than US$7 billion a year. Many argue that this kind of money is available from loans.

Critics of lending money to developing countries argue that there is too much corruption there for the money to be spent effectively. Charities such as Oxfam argue that with proper well-run local schemes, by local people, this problem can be overcome, as in Koya.

After the war in Sierra Leone

Koya is a small town of 4000 displaced people in Sierra Leone, Africa. Few people in the community are literate. The women say that almost none of them went to school at all when they were children.

But the war, and being forced to move, changed their ideas, and fired a passion for education. "The war was senseless, and made everyone poorer, but maybe one good thing has come out of it: everyone wants the girls to read," says one of the village elders.

Packed tight into the six classrooms, separated only by open wattle partitions, are 200 children. They do a three-year course, mornings only, so they can work with their families the rest of the day. The goal is that by the fourth year they will be ready to join the formal education system.

Later this year 16 of their pupils will take the exam for secondary school. The nearest school is five miles away. The village is prepared to build their own school if necessary.

Adapted from The Guardian, *3 April 2000*

The exploitation of children

Slavery around the world

Over 250 million children work around the world today. Many of these are treated poorly or exploited. Of these, over eight million live in slavery. In other words, they have no control over their own lives; they have to obey other people – their owners.

Article 4 of the UDHR states that "No one shall be held in slavery or servitude; slavery and the slave trade shall be prohibited in all their forms."

Yet around the world, in Africa, Asia, and South America, children as young as five or six are forced to work for others, for little or no money.

The problem is particularly bad in the Indian sub-continent. For example, in India, government figures show that over 18 million children under the age of 14 work, many of them in appalling conditions for extraordinarily low wages.

Child slaves endure appalling conditions for little or no reward

Building a future

"My name is Ashique. I am 11 years old and have been working in the brick kilns for the past six years with my father and three brothers. My father borrowed 20 000 rupees (about £400) to pay for my sister's marriage and now we have to work hard to pay off the loan.

I work every day except Sunday. My father, brothers and myself are paid 30 rupees (50p) for every 1000 bricks. We can make around 2500–3000 bricks in a day. Our wage is cut by 50 per cent for loan repayments. We do not understand the loan interest, which seems to be always increasing. We work from around 2am – when it is still dark – until 6 or 7pm in the evening. We have a short rest of half an hour between 7 and 8am. I am given no time to play.

My father sent me to school, but after three months the kiln owner took me out of school and put me back to work. I liked going to school. I liked being free."

From The Changing Face of Slavery, *Anti-Slavery International*

Discuss

Read 'Building a future'. Which of the rights safeguarded by the UN Declaration of the Rights of the Child do you think are being broken here?

The sexual exploitation of children

The **United Nations Commission on Human Rights** estimates that as many as 10 million children around the world are regularly engaged in sex for money.

The commercial exploitation of children is widespread both in more and less economically developed countries. At least one million children, most of them girls, become prostitutes every year.

Poverty, cultural attitudes and inequality between males and females, are factors which contribute to a climate in which sexual exploitation can occur. In some cultures, poor families will provide their son with an education in preference to their daughter. Because there are few employment opportunities for girls with no formal education, many are forced into the sex trade.

Some poverty-stricken families may sell their children into the sex trade for money to survive or to pay off a debt. Vulnerable children – almost always from poor, marginalized or indigenous or ethnic minority families – are often coerced, kidnapped, forced or conned into working as prostitutes.

An agenda for action

An agenda for action was produced at a World Congress Against the Sexual Exploitation of Children in 1996. It was attended by delegates from 119 countries and called on each country to:

● take action to prevent the commercial exploitation of children

● cooperate with other countries and with all sectors of society to protect children from sexual exploitation and from entering the sex trade

● develop and carry out laws that make the sexual exploitation of children a criminal offence

● develop plans and programs to re-integrate exploited children back into society.

In recent times, laws have been introduced by a number of countries, including Australia, the United Kingdom and the United States, which make it illegal for their citizens to have sex with child prostitutes in other countries.

Children's rights in the UK

Democratic rights

Article 21 of the UDHR states that "Everyone has the right to take part in the government of their country, directly or through freely chosen representatives." However, because children are not entitled to vote, they receive no direct representation in many countries, including the United Kingdom. In the UK, the age of majority is 18. That means anyone aged 17 or under is not allowed to vote.

In January 2001 an independent charity called the UK Youth Parliament was established to represent young people between the ages of 11 and 18 democratically.

The Members of the Youth Parliament (MYPs) work locally with their peer group and local government. In addition, MYPs have regular meetings with the MPs, Government and Shadow Cabinet Ministers.

Members of the Youth Parliament at a meeting with Tony Blair

Children at work in the UK

Over two million children under 16 work in the United Kingdom. Common jobs include working in garden stores, on market stalls or doing a paper round. The law says that those aged between 13 and 16 can work up 12 hours a week.

In order to work, you must get a work application form from your school. This has to be signed by the employer, the school and your parent. The local education authority then decides whether to allow this application. Factors considered are: what you will gain from the experience, and whether the work will affect your school work or your health.

GMB takes on pupil exploitation

The GMB Union has revealed that over 750 000 pupils are being exploited in the UK. Many pupils are spending less time on their homework and more time on out-of-school jobs.

Most young people spend 26 hours per week in the classroom, and should be doing 18 hours homework. Yet some are doing up to 12 hours of paid work per week. All this adds up to a total of 56 hours of work and study each week. The health of thousands of pupils is suffering as a result.

Previous studies have found that up to 28 per cent of children said that sometimes they were too tired to do their schoolwork or homework. Some children have been found to be playing truant, in order to undertake paid work.

GMB

Smacking

One issue that has been strongly debated in the UK is the right of parents to smack children. Article 5 states that no one shall be subjected to cruel punishment.

Supporters of smacking argue that parents should have the right to discipline their children as they choose. As a result, although smacking a child under three is illegal in Scotland, it is still legal in England, Wales and Northern Ireland.

Many parents consider a light smack to be an effective (and essential) punishment when a child's behaviour is exceptionally bad

Discuss

1 Read 'GMB takes on pupil exploitation'. Do you think you ought to be allowed to work at the age of 13?

2 The government says 13–14-year-olds can work two hours on a school day, and five hours on a Saturday. If you are 15–16, you can work eight hours on a Saturday. You are not allowed to work before 7am or after 7pm. Do you think these safeguards are enough?

3 "All MPs should hold regular constituency surgeries for children." Do you agree? Give your reasons.

Basic survival needs

Basic survival needs

Standard of living

Article 25 of the Universal Declaration of Human Rights states that "everyone has the right to a standard of living adequate for the health and well-being of themselves and their family, including food, clothing, housing and medical care".

Freedom from hunger?

- The World Bank estimated that in the year 2000, a billion people worldwide suffered from hunger.
- The UN estimates that about 1.3 million of the world's people live in absolute poverty.
- More than 35 per cent (140 million) of Africa's population suffer from hunger on a daily basis.
- About 10 million children each year die of hunger and poverty-related illnesses. In Africa alone; about 10 000 children die every day from malnutrition and lack of health care.

Poverty and deprivation

Human rights must include the ability to survive – that is, having access to the basic means by which to live. And yet despite improvements in overall poverty figures, progress has been uneven and much human deprivation still remains, especially in the developing world.

One of the great achievements of the 20th century, according to a United Nations report, is the dramatic reduction in human poverty. In the southern hemisphere, more than three-quarters of the population can now expect to survive to the age of 40. Infant mortality has been cut by nearly three-fifths. But this still means that:

- 150 million children under five are malnourished
- 507 million people are not expected to survive to age 40
- 1.2 billion people do not have access to safe drinking water
- 2.4 billion people are without access to basic sanitation
- 11 million children die annually from preventable causes.

United Nations Development Programme Reports, 1997–98

Hunger and malnutrition

The word 'hunger' is emotive and imprecise. The over-used expression 'world hunger' conjures up images of starvation, shrunken limbs, staring eyes and begging-bowls. But the truth is that, although malnutrition is almost everywhere among the poor, the traveller in the Third World rarely sees people who are nothing but skin and bone. Only in extreme situations, in Biafra, Bangladesh or the Sahel do these occur in large numbers. The everyday reality of malnutrition in the Third World is less dramatic. It is adults scraping through, physically and mentally fatigued, and vulnerable to illness. It is children – often dying, not so frequently of hunger alone, as hunger working hand in hand with sickness, but more often surviving impaired for life.

Adapted from Inside the Third World by Paul Harrison

Famines

Although natural disasters such as a flood or a drought can bring about famines, they are not the sole cause. An underlying factor is the poverty of the countries in which they occur. The situation may also be made worse by the outbreak of a civil war. Civil wars create internal chaos by destroying transport links, disrupting agriculture and causing people to become refugees. Many of the African countries where famines occurred in the last three decades of the 20th century suffered from civil wars.

Famines are often created by human factors, which have a devastating impact on the people affected

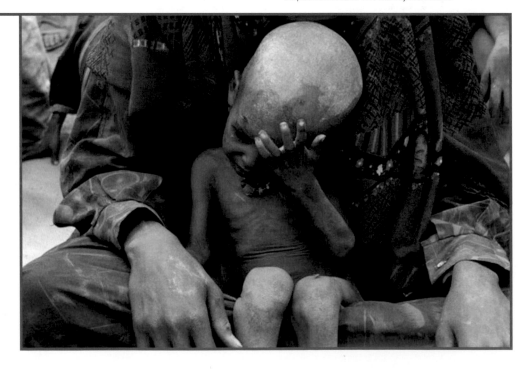

Water

Access to water, like food, is a basic human need. Whereas it is possible for a person to live for up to two weeks without any food, they would only survive for a few days without water.

The water we drink needs to be clean. Many of the illnesses and diseases from which people in the developing world suffer are caused by poor sanitation and a lack of access to clean water.

These African villagers celebrate after their first ever clean water pump is installed

A worldwide water crisis

We are heading for a worldwide water crisis. Already, over 1.2 billion people have no access to safe drinking water. A further 2.5 billion are without sanitation, such as proper drains or sewage systems. Over five million people are killed by waterborne diseases each year.

Fresh water is becoming increasingly hard to obtain. It is so scarce that it may become the main natural resource that limits sustainable development (that is, development which doesn't harm the lives of future generations).

By 2025, about five billion people will be living in water-shortage areas. In other words, it will be difficult or impossible to meet all their needs for fresh water. Amongst these, 2.7 billion people will have little to no supply of drinking water.

This will create "a looming crisis that overshadows nearly two-thirds of the Earth's population", a United Nations report has said.

The problem is that the supply of fresh water is almost fixed. Already, our demand is outstripping world supply. Less than three per cent of the world's water is drinkable fresh water. Most of this is trapped in polar ice, or buried in inaccessible springs deep underground.

This means that freshwater lakes, rivers and reservoirs only contain a very small amount of the world's freshwater supply.

"Even where supplies are sufficient or plentiful, they are increasingly at risk from pollution and rising demand," stated UN Secretary-General Kofi Annan. He added that a shortage of water may lead to more wars and conflicts, as nations fight for limited resources.

Water water everywhere?

Not all countries in the world are affected equally by water shortages. The worst areas are the deserts and semi-arid areas of sub-Saharan Africa and Asia. This is partly because more economically developed countries have higher rainfall than these less economically developed areas. More economically developed areas also have better technology, and make more efficient use of their water resources. Developing countries also have greater population growth, which places a further strain on water resources.

Millions of women in developing countries walk several miles every day to look for water. Alternatively, they send their children to look for it. This limits the amount of time they have to work, grow crops, and attend school, leading to a poverty cycle caused by water shortages.

In developing countries, over 70 per cent of industrial waste, and up to 95 per cent of sewage is dumped into the water supply untreated. This leads to pollution and contamination, further restricting future water supplies.

Many developing countries also use limited sources for their water. The water table in many cities in Asia, South America, and China is dropping by over one metre a year, meaning these sources will eventually dry up.

Water ministers from 22 African countries have called for a global water alliance, to tackle the twin problems of freshwater supplies and sanitation.

One solution is desalinization facilities that turn salt water into fresh water. This is because 97 per cent of the world's water is salty. However, this is too expensive and time consuming for many developing countries. In 2002, treated sea water accounted for less than one per cent of human water consumption.

Environmentalists argue that four things are now necessary:

● protecting water supplies from pollutants
● restoring natural flow patterns to river systems
● managing irrigation and chemical use
● reducing industrial air pollution.

These are all vital steps to improving water quality and availability.

Discuss

1 What do you learn from these pages about the causes of hunger and ill health in the developing world?

2 Discuss ways in which the more economically developed world can help to reduce poverty in less economically developed countries.

Discuss

Read the articles about water shortages. What do you learn about the water crisis? Which countries are most affected? What can be done to tackle water and sanitation problems?

Social rights

The right to security

Article 25 of the Universal Declaration of Human Rights states that in addition to adequate food, clothing, housing and medical care, everyone has the right to security in the event of unemployment, sickness, disability, widowhood, old age, or lack of livelihood in circumstances beyond their control. It specifies, "motherhood and childhood are entitled to special care and assistance".

What is poverty?

What constitutes poverty is relative to the conditions in which the rest of the people in a society are living. Although there is some very real poverty in the UK today, many of today's poor live in conditions that are much better than the conditions poor people lived in 100 years ago.

Similarly, poverty in Africa is very different from poverty in the UK. Many of the world's poorest people have to survive on incomes much lower than those of Britain's poor. 1.2 billion people survive on less than US$1 per day, and 2.8 billion people survive on less than US$2 per day in the world today.

Discuss

Have people with low incomes a right to income support? Or should they have to work in order to receive welfare? Should people with more money and jobs have to pay higher taxes, to help eliminate poverty in the UK? Give reasons for your views.

Poverty and deprivation

The UK is a wealthy country. The majority of the population enjoys a good standard of living. However, there is a considerable minority who are deprived of their social rights through poverty.

People who have very low incomes and few material possessions are regarded as poor. Those with very low incomes receive a payment from the government known as income support. Many people who receive income support find it hard to provide themselves with basic essentials.

"You can't do as much, and I don't like my clothes and that, so I don't really get to do much or do stuff like my friends are doing... I am worried about what people think of me, like they think I am sad or something." Nicole, aged 13

Child Poverty Action Group (www.cpag.org.uk)

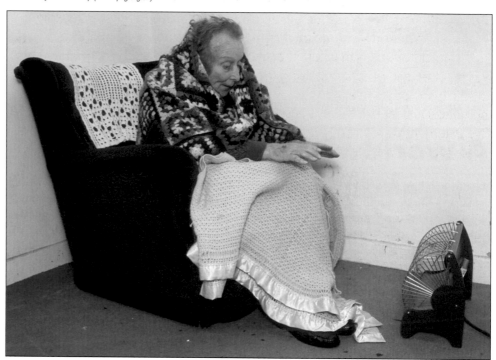

Many of the poorest people in Britain are older people

UK poverty facts

One widely-used definition of poverty is having to survive on less than 50 per cent of the average income, once housing costs have been deducted. According to this definition:

- 1 in 4 people (14.3 million) in the UK were living in poverty in 1998/9 compared with less than 1 in 10 in 1979
- children are even more likely than any other group to be living in poverty – more than 1 in 4 children (3.9 million) were living in poverty in 2000/1 compared with 1 in 10 in 1979.

Different family types face different risks of falling into poverty:

- over half of lone parents (63 per cent) live in poverty
- couples with children account for the largest number of people in poverty (4.9 million).

Homelessness in the UK

Having somewhere to live is a basic **human right**. Yet Shelter, a charity dedicated to helping the homeless, has estimated that there are around 410 000 homeless people in the UK.

People often have a stereotyped picture of a homeless person as someone who has dropped out of society and is sleeping on the street. However, homelessness does not just include those who are sleeping rough. It also includes those in bed and breakfast accommodation, squats and temporary hostels, and private tenants who have no long-term security.

What causes homelessness?

The majority of people who become homeless do not do so out of choice. People become homeless for a wide variety of reasons. Their relationship with their partner may break up and they may have nowhere to go. The relatives or parents with whom they have been living may no longer be willing or able to accommodate them. They may fall behind with their rent or mortgage payments, and be evicted. The reason why they then become homeless is because there is a shortage of affordable homes for them to live in and they are forced into hostels, bed and breakfast accommodation, or to go on the streets.

Homelessness facts

- There are over 1.5 million unfit dwellings in the UK today.
- There are over 800 000 empty homes in the UK. Most of them are privately owned.
- Every week 1000 homes are repossessed in the UK.
- Local authorities spend millions of pounds each year housing homeless households in temporary bed and breakfast accommodation.
- The average annual cost of keeping a family in bed and breakfast accommodation is approximately £11 500.
- A massive shortage of housing is predicted in the UK in 2025, particularly in London and the Southeast of England.

Discuss

"The only way to solve the homeless problem is to build more houses." Do you agree? Give reasons for your views.

Homelessness – a global problem

Experts estimate that there are 100 million people in the world without any shelter at all, sleeping either in the open, in public buildings or in temporary shelters. In addition, there are around 600 million people in the cities of Africa, Asia and Latin America who are living in housing that has no water supply, no proper sanitation and no rubbish collection.

Throughout the world, people become homeless for a number of reasons. Some lose their homes as a result of natural disasters, such as a flood or an earthquake. Others leave their homes because they find themselves in a war zone.

But the majority of people who move do so voluntarily, because they decide to move from the countryside to a city in search of a better life for themselves and their families. However, there are not enough homes in the world's cities for all the people who want to live there.

Even those who manage to get work can find it difficult to find affordable accommodation and often have to live either in cheap boarding houses or in crowded, shared rooms. Many families end up living in shanty towns, in shelters built from any materials they can find. Others have no option but to live on the streets.

Homelessness is not just about people living on the streets. It is also about people who are forced to live in dangerous temporary shelters, because there is nothing else available.

Economic rights

The right to work and full employment

Unemployment and inflation are two of the major problems that face the United Kingdom today. In the 1970s, the Labour government wanted to achieve **full employment**. Full employment is considered to be when 95 per cent of the adult population that is available to work, has a job.

More recent governments have chosen a different approach, which they claim is more realistic. In the 1980s and early 1990s, the Conservative governments concentrated on limiting inflation as their first priority. They were concerned with keeping prices down, so that business could thrive. This would in turn increase the UK's economy and create a better standard of living. However, it is not always possible to have low inflation and full employment.

The current Labour government stresses that they want a situation of full employability, where people are fully trained up for work.

Section 1 of Article 23 of the Universal Declaration of Human Rights goes further. It states, "Everyone has the right to work, to a free choice of employment, to just and favourable conditions of work and to protection against unemployment." This means that unemployment benefit is regarded as a human right, as is the right to work.

Living wage reduces poverty

Home health care worker Claudia Arevalo says her life changed for the better in 2000, when San Francisco enacted its living wage law. A living wage is higher than a **minimum wage** – in simple terms, it allows people to 'live' rather than to 'get by'.

In 1998 Claudia earned $6 an hour, rented out a room in her apartment and worked 300-hour months, which included night shifts as a janitor. Now Claudia, 37, works a regular schedule.

According to a national study, she isn't alone. Cities like San Francisco, that boost minimum wages, are reducing poverty rates for the working poor although, at the same time, they increase unemployment, the study says.

San Francisco's living wage of $10 an hour is about 50 per cent higher than the state's $6.75 minimum wage. Over a 2000-hour work year, that could mean a $6500 raise to $20 000 – and the difference between official poverty and a lifestyle less desperate.

However, there are losers too. According to the report, the 10 per cent of workers who earn the least in areas where the minimum wage is introduced may experience a seven per cent increase in unemployment.

Adapted from the Associated Press

Equal pay for equal work

Young workers in the UK are currently not entitled to the minimum wage unless they are over 18 years old

Since 1997, the UK has had a minimum wage. In early 2002, this was £4.10 an hour, but only if you were over 21. If you were between 18 and 21, the minimum wage was less – £3.50. There was no minimum wage for those working under the age of 18.

Some people disagree with the government, arguing that there should be a minimum wage for everyone, whatever their age. Critics of this idea, including the Conservative party, argue that it would cost young people jobs, and make youth unemployment, already bad in many inner cities, worse.

Meanwhile, Article 23 of the Universal Declaration of Human Rights says that everyone, without any **discrimination**, has the right to equal pay for equal work. In other words, everyone doing the same job should be paid the same, whatever their age.

Discuss

1 Read 'Living wage reduces poverty'. What do you think is more important – bringing people out of poverty, or reducing unemployment? Give reasons for your views.

2 Do you think there should be a minimum wage for young people? Or do you think they should be paid less because of their lack of experience? Give reasons for your views.

A basic standard of living

Article 23 of the Universal Declaration also sets the right to a basic standard of living. It states:

Everyone who works has the right to just and favourable remuneration ensuring for themselves and their family an existence worthy of human dignity, and supplemented, if necessary, by other means of social protection.

This supports the idea of a minimum wage and social security (see page 12). However, there is strong debate about company directors giving themselves large wage rises, while their employees receive wage rises below the rate of inflation. Such directors have been called 'fat cats' by their opponents.

Discuss

Do you think that there should be a legal limit to the size of pay rises that company directors receive? Or should businesses be left alone? Give reasons for your views.

Trade unions

Article 23 also deals with the right to form and join a **trade union**: "Everyone has the right to form and to join trade unions for the protection of their interests."

However, several groups of government workers are not allowed to go on strike. This includes members of the armed forces and the police. In 2001 and early 2002, there was considerable disagreement between the government and the police over reform of the police service. As a result, the police held several high-profile demonstrations in London. However, they could not exercise the right to strike.

In June 2002, a group of air traffic controllers went on strike across Europe, to complain about proposed changes in the industry. The controllers caused chaos to thousands of holidaymakers wishing to travel across Europe. The controllers argued that this was the only way of getting their point across. Critics of the strike argued that this strike damaged everyone's right to freedom of movement across national borders.

Absolute disgrace

At the TUC conference, Roger Lyons, general secretary of the Manufacturing Science and Finance Union, is leading calls for new legislation to restrict big pay-offs to 'fat cats'.

He said: "Payments like this – for failure – are an absolute disgrace. It is the worst kind of fat cattery in the history of British industry. There needs to be some form of sanctions to prevent businessmen who put thousands of jobs at risk from taking lottery-sized payouts as reward for failure."

Trade Secretary, Ms Hewitt, said business leaders behind big success were entitled to big rewards. "But when you've got people losing their jobs and investors losing their money, they ought to be sharing the pain. Failing executives should not be getting the kind of rewards that some of them are getting and some of them are taking." However, she added that it was up to each company's board and shareholders to prevent such episodes.

Corporate duty

During a speech in Manchester, Foreign Secretary Jack Straw, said he did not approve of such pay-outs and would vote against them if he was a shareholder. There was a role for governments, he said, continuing, "We must do what we can to encourage corporate responsibility: we cannot leave companies to regulate themselves globally, any more than we do in our national economies." He said, "I think it's very damaging for the reputation of business in this country for such things to happen… I think what we will see from this case is increasingly companies recognizing their corporate responsibility, if you like, their enlightened self interest."

The police demonstrating at Westminster

Discuss

1 Do you think the police should have the right to strike? Or are the police too important as a public service to be allowed this power? Give reasons for your views.

2 "The right to strike should be taken away from all key public workers, so that innocent people are not caught up in the dispute, and that their rights are protected." Do you agree?

Women's rights

Equal opportunities

Equal opportunities mean that everyone should have the same chances, regardless of any personal factors such as ethnicity, gender or if they are disabled.

Equal opportunities demand an absence of **discrimination**. However, sexual discrimination still often occurs in the United Kingdom. There are a few cases of men being discriminated against because of their sex, but the vast majority of sexual discrimination occurs against women. This is clearly against the law, which is set out in the 1986 Sex Discrimination Act.

The struggle for equal opportunities and equality for women goes back a long time. It was only as recently as 1928 that women were first given the right to vote. Despite this, only one in eight MPs is a woman.

The Equal Opportunities Commission

The **Equal Opportunities Commission** exists to fight discrimination and promote equal opportunities in the UK. It undertakes research on discrimination in the UK. It can complain against any advert or practice that it thinks is discriminatory. It also takes companies and individuals to court when they are breaking the law.

Its powers were strengthened in 1998 when the UK adopted the European Convention on Human Rights into law (see page 3). However, some groups have argued the Equal Opportunities Commission should become part of a Human Rights Commission.

Sexual discrimination in the UK

Sexual discrimination is still a large problem in the United Kingdom today. This is most obvious in the differing rates of pay for women and men. The UDHR states, "Everyone, without discrimination, has the right to equal pay for equal work" (Article 23). However, this is clearly not occurring.

As the chart shows, the problem applies to both manual and non-manual workers. Manual workers are people whose jobs involve physical labour, such as bricklayers, plumbers and gardeners. Non-manual workers include people who work in the service sector of the economy, such as telesales staff, shop assistants and office workers.

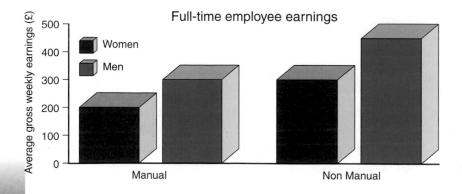

Full-time employee earnings

Average gross weekly earnings (£): 0, 100, 200, 300, 400, 500

Women
Men

Manual   Non Manual

Discrimination and sexual harassment

Discrimination may take two forms – direct discrimination and indirect discrimination. Direct discrimination is when an employer treats a member of one sex less favourably than that of another. Recent examples include a female banker being paid a smaller bonus than her male colleagues, and a male barman who was sacked for having a ponytail, even though his female colleagues were allowed long hair.

One form of direct discrimination is sexual harassment. This is defined as "unwanted conduct of a sexual nature or other conduct affecting the dignity of men and women at work". This can include physical contact, verbal or non-verbal conduct.

Indirect discrimination is more difficult to define and prove. Indirect sexual discrimination occurs when a set of rules discriminate unfairly against one sex over another. For example, if a factory imposes irregular shifts on its employees, this may indirectly discriminate against female employees with young families.

There are, however, some exemptions from discrimination regulations. For example, there is a minimum height requirement for people wishing to join the police. This may discriminate against women, who are shorter on average than men.

Discuss

Many employers have a code of conduct, which tells their employees how to behave. Imagine you were creating a code of conduct for your school. What would you include to prevent sexual discrimination, and in particular, sexual harassment from occurring?

Other forms of sexual discrimination

Sexual discrimination does not just involve the level of women's pay. There is also a failure of people to understand women's issues. This can be connected to any number of subjects, including **childcare**, retirement and what jobs women do.

Childcare is when a person looks after a parent's child, usually so they can go out to work. When childcare facilities are not present, it often indirectly discriminates against mothers who wish to work. Among those institutions which have been criticized for poor childcare facilities is the House of Commons, which has a large number of bars, but no room for a crèche or playgroup for the children of MPs. This is often a problem for women.

Sexual discrimination doesn't just affect women at work – it carries on when they retire. About two-thirds of women live on or below the income support level in poverty (see page 10). This means that they are unable to participate in society, and are discriminated against in old age.

Research shows...

Many women still wish for a man to be the boss. Research in 1998 by the Pitman Group showed that 82 per cent of men and 86 per cent of women dislike being subordinate to a woman. In Scotland the combined figure was as high as 95 per cent.

Discuss

Do you think we should respect people's views, and keep male bosses? Or does a lot more work need to be done in the area of equal opportunities? Give reasons for your views.

Women will not be frontline troops

Women will not be allowed to fight with frontline units in the British military, Geoff Hoon, the Defence Secretary, will announce next month.

The argument over whether women should be allowed to join units such as the Parachute Regiment, SAS, marines, and armoured regiments has been running since Labour took office in 1997.

Hoon will announce that women will continue to be barred from roles where close-quarter fighting with the enemy is likely.

At present 73 per cent of navy jobs are open to women. In the army the figure is 70 per cent, whilst in the RAF 96 per cent of jobs are available to women, including piloting fighter jets.

Women can still serve in a war zone, with a number currently in Afghanistan, but they are excluded from units whose role it is to engage with the enemy.

A report on the issue, written by the army last summer on behalf of all three services, showed that while some exceptional female candidates could manage frontline roles, most are not physically up to the job.

The report's authors carried out a host of physical tests on groups of male and female soldiers. While the cohesion of mixed-sex units suffered slightly, the report found stark differences in performance. Tests also showed that the injury rate among women was double that of male soldiers.

However, the Ministry of Defence is preparing for a legal challenge. Lawyers have advised that a case could be brought under the European Convention of Human Rights, if an applicant claimed she was denied a job because of her gender.

Although women are welcomed into the armed forces, they are not allowed to enter into frontline combat

Adapted from the Sunday Times, 27 January 2002

Discuss

1 Read, 'Women will not be frontline troops.' Do you think the armed forces are guilty of direct or indirect discrimination? Give reasons for your views.

2 Article 23 of the Universal Declaration of Human Rights states "Everyone has the right to work". But is childcare a human right? Some people have argued that it is, however opponents of this view ask why the state should pay for childcare. Give reasons for your views.

The right to life or the right to choose?

Abortion

Article 6 of the **UN Convention on the Rights of the Child** states, "Every child has the inherent right to life, and the state has an obligation to ensure the child's survival and development."

Every day one million women become pregnant. Fifty per cent of women do this by accident. Of these pregnancies, 25 per cent are ended when the women choose to have their pregnancy terminated. This is known as an **abortion**.

People's opinions on abortion vary widely. Pro-life groups believe that abortion kills a human being, and so is morally wrong under any circumstances. Pro-choice groups believe that it is the right of individual women to choose whether to continue with a pregnancy, depending on her beliefs, attitudes and circumstances.

Abortion in the UK

For hundreds of years, abortion was illegal in the UK, except in very exceptional circumstances. Nevertheless thousands of abortions were carried out annually by so-called 'back-street abortionists'.

In 1967, the Abortion Act was passed. This made it legal for a pregnancy to be terminated in England, Scotland and Wales, by a doctor, if two or more doctors certify that:

- to continue the pregnancy would involve a greater risk to the life or physical or mental health of the mother or her existing children, than to terminate it
- there is a substantial risk that if the child was born it would be seriously physically or mentally handicapped.

The 1967 Act was linked to a 1929 Act that made it a criminal offence to destroy the life of a foetus capable of being born alive. At the time this was considered to be when the foetus was 28 weeks old. In 1990 the time limit was reduced to 24 weeks. In some exceptional circumstances, to save the life of the mother, abortion is allowed up to 40 weeks.

In 2000, there were 175 542 abortions, or almost 17 abortions per 1000 women aged 15–44 in England and Wales. Of these, 21 per cent were for teenagers aged 19 or below. England and Wales have one of the highest teenage pregnancy rates in the whole of Europe.

Abortion in Europe

- ■ Abortion permitted only to save a woman's life
- ■ As above plus to preserve the woman's physical or mental health
- □ As above plus for economic or social reasons
- ■ Abortion permitted on request

Abortion in Europe

Abortion in Ireland and Northern Ireland

The 1967 Abortion Act in the UK excluded Northern Ireland. Currently, the law in Northern Ireland is very confusing for abortions during the first 27 weeks in a pregnancy (termination is allowed after 28 weeks only to save the life of the mother). This means that doctors have to make their own decisions, and hope that they are legal. In practice, abortion has been allowed in Northern Ireland under the following conditions:

- if abnormalities of the foetus are detected
- if the woman has a serious medical or psychological problem which could threaten her health or her life if the pregnancy continued
- if the woman has severe learning difficulties.

South of the border, in Ireland, abortion is only allowed in extreme circumstances to save a mother's life. As a result, some 6000 Irish women travel to the UK each year for an abortion. Meanwhile, the majority of European countries have made abortion available on demand. In other words, a woman can simply choose to have an abortion in the early stages of pregnancy.

Discuss

Do you think abortion should be allowed on demand? Or should we allow abortion only when a mother's life is in serious danger, as in Ireland? Give reasons for your views.

The right to choose

Pro-choice groups that support the right for women to choose include the National Abortion Campaign, and the Pregnancy Advisory Service. Both groups argue that abortion should be allowed because:

- a pregnant woman is the best person to make any decision about a pregnancy
- there is no form of contraception that is 100 per cent safe
- public opinion supports legal abortion
- where abortion is illegal, such as in Ireland, women still travel to a country where abortion is legal, and have the abortion anyway.

Pro-life groups include LIFE, and SPUC, the Society for the Protection of the Unborn Child. These groups argue that abortions are immoral, and should be prevented, because:

- human life begins at conception, and every abortion destroys a human being
- abortions performed because a foetus is abnormal is the worst form of discrimination against disabled people
- abortion damages women, because they may suffer trauma, guilt, and depression – sometimes for years afterwards
- there are alternatives to abortion, such as adoption.

These demonstrators believe the rights of the unborn child are more important, and that abortion should be made illegal. There are also many supporters of the opposing viewpoint that abortion should be a right for every woman.

Abortion facts

In 1973 the American Constitution was amended to allow abortion.

In Latin America, where abortion is almost completely illegal, it is estimated that the rate of abortions is between 30 and 60 per thousand women each year. This compares with a Western European average of 14 per thousand.

In China's cities, a one-child policy means that abortion is compulsory in the event of a second pregnancy. In the countryside those who have a daughter first may try again for a son. After that they must terminate all pregnancies. There are at least 10 million abortions in China every year.

Discuss

"No one has the right to force anyone to have an abortion. China's one-child policy is an abuse of human rights." Do you agree with this statement? Give reasons for your views.

When life begins

A key factor influencing a person's views on abortion is their view on when life begins. Does life begin:

- at the moment of conception
- at the point during pregnancy when the baby – if born prematurely – could sustain life outside the womb
- at the moment of birth?

Discuss

"The unborn child has rights which must be protected at all costs. Governments should legislate to ensure these rights are enforced." Do you agree or disagree with this view? Why?

Public opinion

Whether or not you support abortion can depend very much on the circumstances. In 1998, a case in Ireland caused a wide debate on whether a 13-year-old rape victim should be allowed an abortion, due to exceptional circumstances.

The table below shows the results of an opinion poll, on the British public's attitudes towards abortion under different circumstances:

Do you approve or disapprove of abortion under the following circumstances?			
	Approve	Disapprove	Don't know
Where the mother's life is endangered by the pregnancy	93%	3%	4%
Where the mother's health is at risk by the pregnancy	88%	6%	6%
Where the woman has been raped	88%	6%	6%
Where it is likely that the child would be born mentally handicapped or mentally disabled	67%	20%	13%
Where it is likely that the child would be born physically handicapped or physically disabled	66%	21%	13%
Where the woman is under the age of consent (16)	58%	29%	13%

MORI/British Pregnancy Advisory Service 1997

Racism

Racial discrimination

Racial **discrimination**, or racism, is when a person is discriminated against because of their skin colour, their ethnic origin or the country they come from. Racism is an increasing problem in many European countries. In 2002, for example, during local council elections in the UK, the racist British National Party succeeded in winning three council seats in Burnley in the Northwest of England.

Racial discrimination can manifest itself in many different ways. It includes racial violence, such as attacks and muggings against individuals. Racial tension was to blame for riots in Burnley and Oldham in 2001.

Racial discrimination can also lead to a lack of job opportunities, a person being denied promotion or sacked from work, merely because of their skin colour. It also includes racial harassment, whether this is by individuals, or even by government agencies.

In 1976 Parliament passed the Race Relations Act making racial discrimination unlawful in areas such as employment, education, the provision of goods and services, and housing. However, proving discrimination can be difficult.

When allowed to build up, racial tensions often boil over into rioting behaviour, as seen in Burnley and Oldham in 2001

Racism and rights

Two articles of the Universal Declaration of Human Rights deal with racism. Article 6 states, "Everyone has the right to recognition everywhere as a person before the law." There is also Article 7, which states, "All are equal before the law and are entitled without any discrimination to equal protection of the law."

Discuss

1 "It's only natural for people to love their country and not like outsiders." What do you think?

2 Are all wars basically 'ethnic' or 'racial' conflicts? Explain the reasons for your answer.

Adapted from "Racism" by Jagdish Gundara and Roger Hewitt Evans Brothers 1999

Racism and nationalism

Racism is sometimes associated with nationalism – a strong belief in the importance of one's own country. Attachment to our own country can be a perfectly good thing. On the other hand, it has often been the cause of wars as countries compete for dominance and influence in the world. Unfortunately it is also often bound up with beliefs about who should be counted as a member of a country and who should not – who's in and who should be kept out.

Many modern states have developed out of groups of much smaller countries where people tended to speak the same or similar languages. In the mid-19th century, for example, neither Italy nor Germany existed as single countries, but were formed from a number of small self-governing states. Where one country ends and another begins seems fairly simple when the country is also an island, but quite often it is just a matter of chance as to where a line gets drawn between two countries. Those who are 'in' and those who are 'out' might be very similar, even identical to each other.

Most countries are actually made up of many different ethnic groups.

People come to feel that they are attached to a certain country by where they and other members of their family were born. They feel themselves to be part of the history and culture of that country. Sometimes this way of identifying with a country leads people into thinking that some people have more of a right to belong than others.

In countries where several ethnic groups live in little pockets near each other – such as in the area formerly known as Yugoslavia – conflicts can arise that lead to wars and to the expelling of those who suddenly find themselves regarded as 'outsiders' when a new government draws the line around the country in a new way.

Removing those who are no longer considered as belonging has sometimes been called 'ethnic cleansing'. In the name of ethnic cleansing, people have been driven from their homes, imprisoned, tortured and executed. It is exactly this kind of discrimination, **prejudice** and cruelty that marks it out as a form of racism.

Our multicultural nation

The UK has a population of 57.1 million. Of this population, 53 million are white and four million are from an ethnic minority. The people from an ethnic minority have various ethnic origins, although it is important to remember that 50 per cent of ethnic minority citizens were born in the UK.

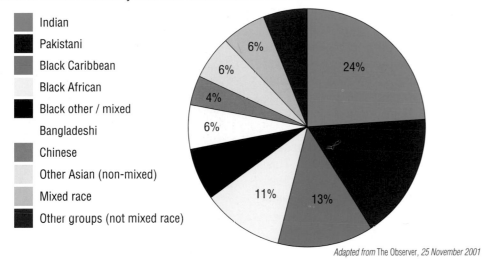

- Indian
- Pakistani
- Black Caribbean
- Black African
- Black other / mixed
- Bangladeshi
- Chinese
- Other Asian (non-mixed)
- Mixed race
- Other groups (not mixed race)

Adapted from The Observer, *25 November 2001*

Institutional racism

A report into the police handling of the investigation into the murder of black teenager Stephen Lawrence by a gang of white youths, stated that police incompetence and institutional racism had hindered the search for the killers, who have never been brought to justice.

The report, known as the Macpherson Report, defined institutional racism as, "The collective failure of an organization to provide an appropriate and professional service to people because of their colour, culture or ethnic origin. It can be seen or detected in processes, attitudes and behaviour which amount to discrimination through unwitting prejudice, ignorance, thoughtlessness and racist stereotyping which disadvantage minority ethnic people."

In 2000, in an effort to eradicate institutional racism, Parliament passed another Race Relations Act extending the law to make indirect discrimination unlawful throughout the public services. This covers public bodies such as the police, prisons, schools and hospitals.

Is the Commission for Racial Equality outdated?

The **Commission for Racial Equality (CRE)** exists to fight racial discrimination. The CRE undertakes research on racism in the UK and works with public organizations to ensure equal treatment for all. It also provides information and advice to people who think they have suffered racial discrimination, and makes sure all new laws take full account of the Race Relations Act.

Following devolution, Northern Ireland set up a full Human Rights Commission. This looks into all areas of human rights abuses, including racism, sexism (see pages 14–15) and discrimination against people with disabilities (see page 20). The Welsh Assembly has also created a Human Rights Commission, and the Scottish Parliament has done the same. However, London and England still only have separate bodies dealing with separate areas.

Human rights groups argue that we need a full Human Rights Commission for England, and especially London, where half of the UK's four million members of ethnic minorities live. For example, when a black woman with a disability is discriminated against, why is she being discriminated against? Is it because she is black? Or that she is a woman? Or that she is disabled? A Human Rights Commission would be able to investigate all of these areas.

Lawrence report lessons being ignored by police

Police chiefs are ignoring one of the Stephen Lawrence inquiry report's main recommendations – to provide racial diversity training for all staff – and are failing to promote ethnic minority officers, government inspectors will reveal today.

Many forces have also been criticized for not bothering to check whether they are stopping and searching a disproportionate number of black and Asian people.

On the controversial issue of stop and search, which has come under attack because there are more searches on black and Asian people, the inspectors say there is a general complacency among most forces about how this technique is used.

The Independent, *6 October 2002*

The police are entitled to stop individuals and search them, but individuals must not be targeted on racial grounds

Discuss

1 What is meant by institutional racism and what can its effects be?

2 Do you think there should be a fully independent Human Rights Commission to coordinate work in the UK on all areas of human rights? Give reasons for your views.

Disability rights

What is disability?

A person with a **disability** is anyone who has a physical or mental impairment, which considerably affects their ability to carry out day-to-day activities. This includes physical impairments such as blindness, deafness, severe disfigurement, or the loss or paralysis of a limb. Mental impairments include learning difficulties, such as problems remembering facts or faces, or trouble communicating with people. Mental impairments also include all recognized mental illnesses, such as schizophrenia and depression. It is estimated that there are over 8.5 million people with disabilities in the UK.

The Universal Declaration of Human Rights states that these people have as much right to participate in the community as everyone else. In particular, Article 22 states that:

Everyone, as a member of society, has the right to social security and is entitled to realization, through national effort and international cooperation and in accordance with the organization and resources of each state, of the economic, social and cultural rights indispensable for their dignity and the free development of their personality.

However, there are often barriers in place which prevent people with disabilities from participating fully in the community. These barriers can include doors too narrow to allow a wheelchair through, or text so small in a newspaper that a partially-sighted person cannot read it.

In 1995, the government passed the Disability Discrimination Act. This makes it unlawful for a person with a disability to be **discriminated** against in the areas of:

- employment
- access to goods, facilities and services
- the management, buying or renting of land or property.

These rights have also been extended with the passing of the Human Rights Act in 1998 (see page 3). In 2002, a bill was introduced into Parliament, expanding the definition of disability to include those with cancer and HIV. And from 2004, businesses will have to make reasonable adjustments to the physical features of their premises for people with disabilities. This could include access ramps for wheelchairs, hearing loops, and colour coding lines in large buildings to assist the partially sighted.

(see page 3)

Disability and education – the facts

- People with disabilities are twice as likely to have no qualifications as the rest of the population.
- One in five pupils will be identified as having a 'special educational need' while at school.
- One in 20 people with a disability are at a college of further or higher education or university – compared to one in ten of the rest of the population
- More than double the number of people with disabilities are out of work compared to people without a disability.

Many schools integrate pupils with disabilities with able-bodied pupils

Discuss

"Disabled people have around £40 million a year to spend – a fact that businesses and service providers need to bear in mind." Bert Massie, Chair of the Disability Rights Commission.

Imagine you were in charge of a supermarket in your local area. What facilities would you include to ensure equal access for people with disabilities?

The Disability Rights Commission

In 1999, the government created the Disability Rights Commission. This exists to enforce the rights of people with disabilities. It has the power to conduct formal investigations, serve notices on organizations that are breaking the law, and it gives advice to people with disabilities to protect their human rights. The Commission also creates codes of practice for employers to follow for the rights of people with disabilities. It additionally helps resolve disputes over disability rights between employers and employees.

In 2002, the Commission was asked to conduct a review of the Disability Rights Act by the government. The main question the Commission has been asked is, "Do disability rights go far enough?" At the end of this review, the Commission will produce a report for the government, which will then consider making new laws to protect the rights of people with disabilities.

Discuss

Do you think that students with mental impairments are discriminated against more than those with physical impairments? Give reasons for your views.

Homosexual discrimination

Homosexuality

A homosexual is someone who is sexually attracted to people of the same sex. Men who are sexually attracted to men are called gay. Women who are attracted to women are called lesbians. Bisexuals are people who are attracted to both men and women.

The age of consent

The United Kingdom has a legal **age of consent**. This is the age at which people are allowed to have sex. For all couples, the age of consent is 16 in England, Scotland and Wales, and 17 in Northern Ireland.

Originally, the age of consent for homosexual couples was 21. It was reduced to 18 in 1994. Then, in 1997, the pressure group Stonewall successfully took the UK government to European Court (see page 3). The court agreed that the UK's unequal age of consent laws were in violation of the **European Convention on Human Rights**.

In 2000, the government reduced the age of consent to 16 for homosexual couples (17 in Northern Ireland).

The right to marry?

In the UK, marriage brings distinct economic and social advantages. These can include certain forms of tax relief, legal rights for a spouse when no will is made, and receiving priority in council house allocation and benefits.

However, homosexual couples are not allowed to marry in the UK and in much of the Western world. Ceremonies are now legal in San Francisco, but are not always recognized elsewhere. Groups such as Stonewall argue that gay men and lesbians should have the right to marry a same-sex partner and be treated as equal members of society. Opponents of same-sex marriages argue that marriage should only occur between a man and a woman and that therefore Article 16 of the Universal Declaration of Human Rights, about the right to marry, does not apply.

Clause 28

Clause 28 of the Local Government Act 1988 states that any local authority, including schools, shall not:

- intentionally promote homosexuality or publish material with the intention of promoting homosexuality
- promote the teaching of the acceptability of homosexuality as a family relationship in any school.

In 2000, the Scottish Parliament voted to abolish this law in Scotland. It has never existed in Northern Ireland.

Gay pressure groups and others have argued that Clause 28 prevents their right to freedom of speech, as set out in Article 19 of the Universal Declaration of Human Rights. They argue that they should be allowed to produce their own materials freely, and have a right to express their opinions.

However, supporters of Clause 28 argue that without it, unbalanced views of homosexuality could be promoted and influence people, particularly young people, and encourage them to live a homosexual lifestyle. Clause 28, for its supporters, means everyone can make up their own minds because they receive a balanced picture of homosexuality.

Discuss

Do you think Clause 28 should be scrapped in England and Wales? Or should there be some restriction on material and information about homosexuality? Give reasons for your views.

Equal at work?

Article 7 of the UDHR also means that nobody should be discriminated against at work. One particular area of controversy has been the armed forces, where homosexuality is banned, both in the UK and the USA.

In the USA, a person must immediately leave the military if they publicly declare themselves to be homosexual. This is known as 'coming out'. In 2001, the US military dismissed 1250 people from the military, for declaring they were homosexual. This is the highest figure since 1987.

In the UK, two major cases have been taken to the European Court of Human Rights. In both cases, the European Court ruled that the United Kingdom was acting illegally. However, the ban on homosexuals remains in place. Military chiefs argue that to allow homosexuals into the armed forces would reduce the UK's military effectiveness in combat. However, pressure groups such as Stonewall have argued that this is blatant discrimination and that homosexuals should be allowed to serve in the military.

Despite contrary rulings by the European Court of Human Rights, the UK government still does not allow homosexuals to serve in the military

Discuss

1 Do you think homosexuals should be allowed in the UK's armed forces? Give reasons for your views.

2 Should homosexual marriage be legalized in the United Kingdom? Are the human rights of homosexual couples being abused at the moment? What do you think? Give reasons for your views.

Immigration and asylum seekers

What is an immigrant?

An **immigrant** is somebody who arrives to live permanently in a new country. Immigrants are called 'voluntary' when they leave their home country through choice. However, some immigrants are forced to leave their home country by oppressive governments. This goes against Article 9 of the Universal Declaration of Human Rights, which states, "No one shall be subjected to arbitrary arrest, detention, or exile."

Some people migrate from their home countries for negative reasons, known as push factors. Push factors include **persecution**, disease, famine, political instability and torture. Others migrate for positive reasons – to be reunited with their families, because the standard of living is better in the new country, or because there is more chance of finding a job. These are known as pull factors.

Immigrants who arrive in a country looking for better jobs and living conditions voluntarily are known as economic migrants. Often, countries refuse to allow people the right of entry purely for economic reasons. This is particularly the case in times of high unemployment.

Who wins from immigration?

With increasing numbers of people immigrating to the UK, the issue has grown in political importance in recent years. Many people against further immigration feel it will lead to greater social problems, including more crime and lawlessness.

Most of the debate about immigration concerns the cost and benefits to the United Kingdom. Opponents of further immigration argue that economic migrants are taking the jobs of UK citizens, and will work for lower wages. Supporters of immigration argue that there are long-term benefits by letting in skilled workers to fill vacancies where there is a skills gap.

In the European Union, average immigration is about 1.5 million each year, as opposed to 2.3 million in the USA, which is smaller than the EU. Over five per cent of Europeans are born abroad, compared over 10 per cent in the USA, and over 25 in Australia. Previously, east European countries were the main source of immigrants entering the EU. However, most immigrants now come from African or Asian countries.

There have been both positive and negative effects economically on the UK from immigration. On the negative side, wages have fallen in the lowest-paid jobs as new immigrants often take any work that is available to them. On the positive side, employers gain as wages fall by making more profit. In addition, skills shortages may be met, as the government allows into the UK foreign workers who have skills that are high in demand.

In addition to this, over their lifetime most immigrants pay more in taxes than they receive in benefits. As most immigrants are of working age, they will get jobs in the future and pay tax. They also use fewer health care and educational resources because they are working. Government statistics suggest the growth rate of the economy has been boosted by 0.25 per cent solely as a result of immigration.

Another factor to consider is that in the next 20–30 years, more people will retire than will be born. This means that the proportion of people working will fall and less money will be available to fund people's pensions. Immigration can help offset this by increasing the number of people able to work.

Migration to and from the UK

Many people leave the UK as **emigrants** in contrast to those who arrive as immigrants. An emigrant is the exact opposite of an immigrant – somebody who leaves a particular country to go to live somewhere else. The net effect of people immigrating and emigrating to and from a country is known as migration. Migration has very recently started increasing the population in the UK.

Due to the low birth rate and subsequent ageing population in the UK, the country has a shortage of skilled workers. In 2002, this prompted the Government to discuss introducing a green card visa scheme, similar to the scheme run in the USA. Here, highly-skilled foreign workers are allowed into a country, as this benefits everyone – the employer who fills a long unfulfilled vacancy, the foreign worker who gets a new job, and the government, which gets more taxes.

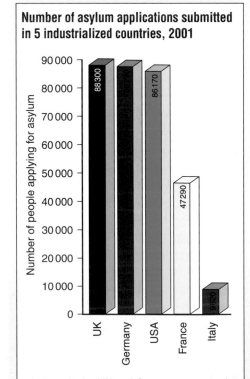

Number of asylum applications submitted in 5 industrialized countries, 2001

Number of people applying for asylum

- UK: 88 300
- Germany:
- USA: 86 170
- France: 47 290
- Italy: 9 620

Although the UK and Germany are much smaller in population than the USA, they received almost the same number of asylum applications.

United Nations Human Rights Commission

Discuss

Read 'Who wins from immigration?' What do you think the main points are for and against immigration? What conditions would you set for immigrants who wish to settle in the UK?

Asylum seekers

Refugees may sometimes apply for **asylum**. This is a form of protection that allows people to stay in a foreign country for their own safety. In the United Kingdom, asylum can be granted for several different reasons. These include:

- political reasons, where asylum is used to protect those people under threat from political persecution

- humanitarian reasons, for example where asylum is granted when young children are in their home country and need to be reunited with their parents, who are in the UK. Asylum is rarely granted on humanitarian grounds.

The right to asylum forms the basis for Article 14 of the Universal Declaration of Human Rights, which states, "Everyone has the right to seek and to enjoy in other countries asylum from persecution."

In order to protect refugees, the United Nations set up the **United Nations High Commissioner for Refugees (UNHCR)** in 1951. The High Commissioner works with charities, such as the Refugee Council in the United Kingdom, to provide help, training and legal advice for refugees all over the world.

The UNHCR also monitors problems in countries and tries to help prevent people from becoming refugees. In 2001, the UNHCR estimated there were 12 million refugees in the world, a decrease from the highest figure of 17.8 million in 1992. However, the UNHCR is concerned about another 19.7 million people who live in trouble spots around the world, and may become refugees in the future.

What is a refugee?

Often, the terms refugee and immigrant get confused. A refugee is someone who has had to flee their country against their wishes as an involuntary emigrant. Often this is due to push factors, such as hunger, the threat of war or political persecution.

Currently, approximately one person in every 500 is a refugee in the UK. This is one of the lowest proportions of refugees in the world. Over one in four people in Jordan are refugees. In France, one person in every two hundred is a refugee.

A common approach?

One problem is the lack of a common approach by EU countries. Different countries have different rules. For example, in France, asylum seekers must wait 12 months before they work. In the UK, this is only six months.

In mid-2002, the 15 EU governments held a summit at Seville in Spain, to try to work out a common asylum and immigration policy.

However, agreement appears to be years away, with different countries enforcing different rules, sometimes in violation of human rights. In Denmark, for example, it is now illegal for someone to marry a foreigner until they are 24. This is to prevent arranged marriages from occurring. However, it acts against a refugee's right to marry.

Illegal immigrants climb out of a truck in Calais, after getting caught trying to sneak across the Channel to Dover

Asylum seekers in the UK

The number of people seeking asylum in the UK has increased in recent years. In 2002, the Home Secretary, David Blunkett, proposed a Nationality, Immigration and Asylum Bill. This bill proposed stricter conditions for people to claim asylum in the UK. The new bill included the following proposals:

- asylum seekers in future would be housed in special centres, possibly on disused military bases, rather than being integrated into the local population

- children seeking asylum would be kept out of local schools, and educated separately, at least while their asylum application was being made

- if an asylum seeker's case was turned down, they could appeal, but only after they had left the country

- in future, those wishing to settle in the UK would be given English and citizenship classes

- there would be tougher security measures and penalties against people trafficking, where illegal immigrants are smuggled into the UK by criminal gangs.

The government says these proposals are necessary in order to reduce the growing problem of immigration. However, pressure groups such as the Refugee Council argue that this may violate a whole variety of human rights, such as the right to freedom of movement, the right to a fair hearing and the right to an education.

Discuss

Look at the proposals in the Nationality, Immigration and Asylum Bill. Do you think any of the proposals violate any human rights? If so, which ones and why? Do you agree with the proposals? Give reasons for your views.

23

Freedom of expression

Can you freely express yourself?

Article 19 of the Universal Declaration states, "Everyone has the right to freedom of expression and opinion." This freedom includes:

- freedom to join, or not to join the army
- freedom to practise one's religious beliefs
- freedom to criticize a government
- freedom to join a political party or a pressure group.

National service and freedom of expression

Some countries support their armies through national, or military, service. In these countries, all men, and sometimes women, above a certain age have to serve in the army for 1–2 years. People on national service are known as conscripts. The UK used to have national service, until 1962.

In Israel, where national service applies to men and women, the issue of national service is a sensitive one. Human rights observers have reported human rights abuses on both sides in the Middle East conflict between Israelis and Palestinians. These reports have included allegations of human rights abuses by the Israeli army, at refugee camps such as Jenin.

As a result, some conscripts have refused to fight for the Israeli army. These conscripts argue that they should be allowed to exercise their freedom of expression in choosing not to fight and so become conscientious objectors.

Palestinian women walk past an Israeli soldier whilst going about their day-to-day business in the West Bank

Freedom of religious belief

A fundamental right in the Universal Declaration is freedom of religious worship. Along with national and cultural differences, religion has been one of the major causes of war and human rights abuses throughout human history and is still a major cause today.

The Universal Declaration specifically mentions religious freedom. Article 18 states, "Everyone has the right to freedom of thought, conscience, and religion; this right includes freedom to change their religion or belief, and freedom to manifest their religion or belief in teaching, practice, worship and observance."

In early 2002, the USA captured many Muslim fundamentalists in Afghanistan. They kept these prisoners at the US army camp at Guantanamo Bay in the Caribbean and imposed very strict security on the prisoners.

At one point, prisoners were not allowed to wear turbans. The treatment of the prisoners was highlighted in the media, and provoked an international outcry. As a result, the USA agreed to allow the Muslim prisoners the right to wear turbans, and the right to pray.

Media freedom

A free media means that the media is allowed to question and criticize the government. In America, the right to **free speech** is so strong that anyone is allowed to set up a TV or radio station and broadcast what they like. This has allowed far-right groups in the USA to publicize racist views on the internet.

However, in many countries around the world, the media are not free. For example, in 2001, Zimbabwe held an election in which many people were not able to vote, and violence and intimidation was widespread. This went against Article 21 of the Universal Declaration, which states that, "Everyone has the right to take part in the government of their country", and that "everyone's vote is equal".

Following criticism from the international media, President Robert Mugabe of Zimbabwe banned foreign journalists from entering and reporting in Zimbabwe. This has severely limited the information coming out of the country.

Discuss

1 What limits should there be on free speech? Should we allow groups to publish and broadcast blasphemous or racist statements? Or should there be more limits on what we can say in public? Give reasons for your views.

2 Do you think national service is a good idea? Or should individuals be allowed the freedom to choose whether to join the army?

Euthanasia and the right to die

The word **euthanasia** comes from two Greek words *eu*, which means good, and *thanatos*, which means death. Literally, euthanasia means the 'good death'. This is when a person chooses to die with dignity, at a time and by a means of their own choice, rather than to suffer.

Active euthanasia

Active euthanasia is when a person chooses to commit suicide, or someone actively helps them, for example by injecting them with lethal drugs designed to kill. In 1995, the Northern Territory in Australia passed a law permitting active euthanasia, for terminally ill patients.

This led to the world's first machine built to legally kill patients. It was never used because the Australian Senate overruled the Northern Territory law, despite opinion polls showing 81 per cent of Australians in favour of euthanasia. Similarly, in Oregon USA, the state legislature passed a law in the 1990s permitting active euthanasia, but the Federal US government overruled it.

Since a legal case in 1997, active euthanasia has been legal in Colombia, provided the patient has clearly given their consent.

In 1995, in Japan, a court in Yokahama found a doctor guilty of murdering a terminally ill cancer patient. As a result of this case, the court then listed four conditions under which euthanasia would be permitted in Japan:

- death is imminent and inevitable for the patient
- the patient is suffering unbearable physical pain
- all possible measures have been taken to relieve pain, and no other treatments are possible
- the patient has clearly expressed their desire to shorten their life.

Euthanasia was made legal in the Netherlands in 2002.

Dr Jack Kevorkan is seen here on trial for creating the first assisted suicide machine. A computer asked the patient three times whether they definitely wanted to die. If the patient agreed all three times, lethal drugs were injected through a needle into the patient's arm. They then slipped into unconsciousness and died within five minutes.

The right to die?

Supporters of euthanasia in the UK include the Liberal Democrats, and the Voluntary Euthanasia Society (VES). The VES argues that freedom of expression should mean a person should be able to have the right to die. This can be done either passively or actively.

Passive euthanasia

Recently, some doctors in the UK have begun to practise passive euthanasia. This is when a patient requests pain-killing drugs primarily to reduce their discomfort. However, such drugs may also reduce a person's lifespan.

Both passive and active euthanasia remain illegal in South Africa. This is despite a survey showing that 12 per cent of South African doctors have already helped terminally ill patients die, usually by passive euthanasia.

Recent cases in the UK

The debate over euthanasia has increased over the last few years. In 2000, a proposed anti-euthanasia bill was defeated in Parliament. The Conservative Party spoke against euthanasia. Its spokesman warned against involuntary euthanasia being practised on elderly hospital patients, to free up hospital beds. The party called for clearer guidelines for medical personnel in the UK.

In early 2002, a 43-year-old paralysed woman known only as Miss B won the right to die. This would involve her being taken from an intensive care ward where she had been kept alive for a year by machines. She would then be taken to doctors who were prepared to switch the machine off. The court allowed this ruling as it would be passive euthanasia, where nature would be allowed to take its course without outside interference.

Discuss

1 Do you think the right to life (Article 3 of the Universal Declaration of Human Rights) is more important than the right to choose to die?

2 Should people be allowed to practise active euthanasia, and if so, under what circumstances? Give reasons for your views.

3 "Passive euthanasia is acceptable, because its primary purpose is to reduce pain and suffering. Forcing people to live longer in pain is a form of torture, and thus contravenes Article 5 of the Universal Declaration (see page 29)." Do you agree with this view?

Human rights abuses

Prevention

Fifty years after the UN Convention on Human Rights was signed, **human rights** are still being abused across the world. This has led to governments increasingly trying to prevent human rights abuses from occurring, rather than just taking action against those responsible after they have occurred.

Politicians argue that strong measures are needed to protect human rights. Solutions that governments have used to deal with human rights abuses include: diplomatic tactics, unarmed observers, peacekeepers, pressure groups, military action and economic sanctions.

Diplomacy

Governments use diplomacy to stop other governments and military groups from abusing human rights. For example, the UK government has successfully intervened in many legal cases of UK citizens sentenced to death abroad (see page 28). Often, but not always, the UK government has managed to pressure foreign governments into reducing a death sentence to life imprisonment.

Unarmed observers

In autumn 1998, many of Europe's governments became concerned by human rights abuses in the Serbian province of Kosovo. They decided to act through a body called the OSCE (the Organization for Security and Cooperation in Europe). The job of the OSCE is to maintain peace and security between the many countries of Europe.

The OSCE sent 2000 unarmed observers to Kosovo to monitor and report any human rights abuses. This was a popular political option, as it complied with UN international law.

However, the observers proved little use, as they had no real power to stop human rights abuses from occurring. In addition, there has always been the danger that observers may be taken hostage by participants in whatever conflict is occurring. As a result, the USA and UK governments decided to take independent military action in Kosovo (see right).

Unarmed observers were also deployed in Israel in early 2002. Again, they had little effect on the cycle of violence between Israel and the Palestinians.

Pressure groups campaigning for change

Groups such as **Amnesty International** run campaigns to draw attention to people who have been wrongly imprisoned abroad, merely for exercising their human rights. These people are known as prisoners of conscience. Amnesty International asks its members to write letters to the government holding the prisoner.

Pressure groups also use the international media to highlight human rights abuses. For example, each year, the pressure group Human Rights Watch publishes a report of human rights abuses that governments have committed. By naming and shaming governments with specific details of human rights abuses, Human Rights Watch hopes to pressure governments into improving human rights in the future.

Military action

Military action means sending in troops, or deploying aircraft to prevent further human rights abuses from occurring. In 1990, in response to Iraq's invasion of Kuwait, a coalition of countries, led by the USA, attacked Iraq. They ultimately forced the Iraqi army to withdraw from Kuwait. This was done with the full authority of the United Nations.

However, in March 1999, a NATO force led by America, with British involvement, subjected Serbian forces to a sustained air bombardment, to prevent further human rights abuses in Kosovo. Serbian troops were forced to withdraw. However, critics of this action point out that this was done without the permission of the United Nations, and that many civilians lost their lives.

Discuss

1 Do you think that the United Nations Commission on Human Rights should have greater powers to intervene in large-scale conflicts where human rights abuses are occurring? Why?

2 Imagine you were faced with a situation where one country had invaded another. Which of the options discussed on these pages would you use to ensure human rights were upheld? Why?

3 Now imagine that a civil war was being fought by two sides within the borders of one country. Would you use any different methods? Why?

4 Do you think the United States has the right to impose trade sanctions against Iraq? Why? Give reasons for your views.

United Nations Peacekeepers

Peacekeepers are sent to areas where there have been human rights abuses, to prevent further problems from occurring. Peacekeepers are from the armies of different UN countries and report to the UN. They wear UN blue helmets or berets to show their neutrality.

Peacekeepers have been both the greatest success and worst disaster for the United Nations. Since 1964, peacekeepers have been stationed in Cyprus. Although they have not provided a political solution to the divided island, they have reduced violence to a low level.

UN peacekeepers may only take action if they are attacked. This led to the UN peacekeepers standing by hopelessly whilst civilians were murdered only a few miles away in Bosnia in the mid-1990s. This, along with similar situations in East Timor in 1999, has led to calls for the UN to be given greater powers to intervene in conflicts.

A member of the UN Peacekeeping Force in East Timor

Trade sanctions imposed by America	Cuba
Trade sanctions imposed by the UN	Iraq
Trade sanctions imposed by the UN in the 1980s	South Africa
Unarmed observers	Israel
Military action	Iraq, Afghanistan, Serbia and Kosovo
Unarmed observers then military action	Bosnia
Peacekeepers	Cyprus and East Timor

Economic sanctions

Economic sanctions are a form of economic pressure. Sanctions mean that a country will refuse to trade certain goods with another country, hurting them economically. Supporters of sanctions argue that they force countries to change their behaviour.

Opponents of sanctions argue that they often affect the very people whose human rights are being abused. Article 25 of the Universal Declaration of Human Rights states, "Everyone has the right to a standard of living adequate for the health and well-being of themselves and their family including medical care."

So far sanctions have had mixed success. Sanctions helped remove the racist South African government in the 1980s. Sanctions currently apply to both Cuba and Iraq. However, medical care has become very restricted in Iraq since sanctions were imposed in the 1990s. In this case, sanctions appear to be hurting and violating the human rights of some of the vulnerable people in Iraqi society, especially children.

Human rights and sanctions – the US versus Iraq

Since the early 1990s, the international community has been suspicious that Saddam Hussein, the military dictator ruling Iraq, has been trying to acquire weapons of mass destruction (see Global Concerns, page 10). This has included the accusation that chemical weapons were used against the Kurds, a minority group who live in northern Iraq.

Because of this and suspicion that Saddam Hussein was using public money for his own purposes, following Iraq's invasion of Kuwait the United Nations voted to use economic sanctions against Iraq. The idea was to force Saddam Hussein to allow UN weapons inspectors free and unlimited access to all and any of Iraq's chemical, biological, and nuclear weapon programmes.

The USA argues that sanctions in Iraq have been a partial success, forcing Saddam Hussein to limit his weapons programmes. However, because of these sanctions, Iraq has faced economic hardship. The standard of living for many ordinary Iraqis has plummeted. Children have died due to a lack of medical supplies, or because their parents cannot afford hospital care.

Meanwhile, the issue of weapons inspection means that in 2002 the USA was considering invading Iraq, which could lead to an all-out war in the region.

Human rights and punishment

Putting human rights abusers on trial

In the past, governments have found it difficult to catch criminals guilty of **human rights** abuses. Often they are protected by foreign governments, or the foreign government itself may be guilty.

In the worst cases of human rights abuse, the United Nations intervenes. In areas where war crimes such as genocide (the widespread killing of a group of people) occurs, the United Nations sets up a war crimes tribunal. This tribunal has the power to call witnesses, demand documents and other evidence, and hold trials.

The first war crimes tribunal occurred immediately after World War II. These were known as the Nuremberg trials, held in Nuremberg in Germany. This court heard cases against Nazi war criminals for atrocities committed during, and leading up to World War II.

More recently, a war crimes tribunal has been investigating cases of genocide in Bosnia and Kosovo in the 1990s. This has resulted in the former Yugoslav leader Slobodan Milosevic being placed on trial at The Hague.

However, overall, the war crimes tribunal has had limited success. The number of people brought to trial doesn't reflect the huge numbers of people killed.

The right to a fair trial

Article 10 of the Universal Declaration of Human Rights states, "Everyone is entitled in full equality to a fair and public hearing by an independent and impartial tribunal, in the determination of their rights and obligations, and of any criminal charge against them."

This means that everyone is entitled to a trial that is unbiased, where strict neutrality according to the law is followed. Unfair trials are among the most common types of human rights abuse, and they occur all over the world.

In its war against terrorism, the USA decided in 2001 that terrorist criminals would be charged and tried by military, not civil courts. This has meant that terrorist trials are held privately. This has led to criticism from human rights groups that terrorist subjects do not receive a fair trial in the USA.

Article 11 of the Universal Declaration states that, "Everyone charged with a penal offence has the right to be presumed innocent until proved guilty."

In 1994, this right was put under threat in the UK by the introduction of a new law. Under arrest, a policeman used to say, "You do not have to say anything, but anything you do say can be taken down and may be used in evidence."

However, with the introduction of the Criminal Justice Act in 1994, your silence can now be used against you in court. A policemen, when arresting someone will now say, "You do not have to say anything, but it may harm your defence if you do not mention when questioned something that you will later rely on in court. Anything you do say may be given in evidence."

A world court

In response to worldwide crime, more than 70 countries have agreed to set up a world court. The world's first International Criminal Court (ICC) started its work in 2002. The idea is that a criminal who has committed a crime in one country can be arrested in another, and be deported back quickly to face trial. The ICC would also be able to hear cases that occurred in countries who have not signed the treaty creating the court. For example, a person committing an offence in Iraq could be charged and tried in the UK, if his actions broke international law.

Supporters of the world court argue that it will bring criminals to trial more quickly, and mean that human rights criminals in other countries will be brought to trial. Critics argue that the court will need more resources to catch criminals, and that countries should place more focus on preventing human rights abuses in the first place. Also, the trials in the ICC need to be in line with people's right to fair trials.

Discuss

1 In 2002, the United States refused to agree to the treaty setting up the International Criminal Court. The United States argued that its own legal system was satisfactory. Do you think the ICC is a good idea? Or should countries simply rely on their own legal systems?

2 Do you think suspected criminals should be entitled to the **right to silence** in the UK? Or should a court be allowed to interpret silence as a sign of guilt?

A terrorist subject held by the USA at Guantanomo Bay. In late 2001 and early 2002, the USA held suspected terrorists without trial for months on end.

The death penalty

Some politicians argue that in order to protect human rights, a strong deterrent is needed. Several countries argue that the strongest deterrent is the death penalty. This is also known as **capital punishment**.

A person who receives the death sentence in the USA has many chances to appeal against the decision. It can take 8–10 years to have somebody executed. Prisoners waiting to hear the result of these appeals are known as being on 'death row'. Human rights campaigners argue that this amounts to mental torture for a long period of time.

Currently, there are over 3400 people in 38 states in America on death row. Since the death penalty was reintroduced in America, over 500 people have been executed.

Article 3 of the Universal Declaration of Human Rights states, "Everyone has the right to life, liberty and security of person." Despite this, the death penalty is still practised in many countries in the world today.

In 2001, over 3000 people were executed in 31 countries, the highest figure for 20 years. The vast majority of these executions occurred in China, where 2468 people were executed in 12 months.

However, by 2002, 111 countries banned the death penalty completely, three more countries than in 2001. This includes the UK, which recently placed a permanent ban on the death penalty, by fully agreeing to the **European Convention on Human Rights** (see page 3).

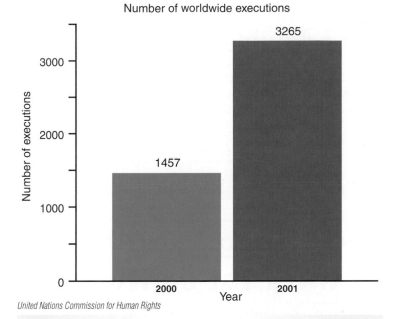

Number of worldwide executions

United Nations Commission for Human Rights

Discuss

Do you think the death penalty abuses Article 3 of the UN Declaration of Human Rights? Or is it necessary for the worst crimes? Give reasons for your views.

Torture

Article 5 of the Universal Declaration states, "No one shall be subjected to **torture**, or to cruel, inhumane, or degrading treatment or punishment." Sadly, torture is still a problem in many countries today. Torture has occurred across much of Africa, Central and South America, the Middle East and Asia over the last 20 years.

Torture is most frequently practised by countries that do not allow political opposition. By silencing their critics, such governments can maintain control and power. Torture can be either physical or mental. Amnesty International has uncovered examples of torture using thumbscrews, electric shocks, racks and red-hot irons.

Mental torture often includes sensory deprivation. This is when a person is prevented from seeing, hearing or feeling. In 1971, sensory deprivation was used in the United Kingdom when 14 men were interrogated by the British security forces. Black hoods like pillowcases were kept over the suspects' heads so they could not see. The suspects were then forced to stand against a wall, with their legs apart and their fingertips against the wall. They were returned to this position by their guards when they fell over. They remained in this position for 16 hours.

Many human rights groups now distinguish between fair and unfair interrogation. Fair interrogation includes detailed questions concerning a crime a person may have committed.

Torture has been widely used in Chinese-occupied Tibet, with many Tibetan Buddhist monks and nuns amongst the victims. Here, Palden Gyatso, a Tibetan monk, displays instruments of torture used on him in prison by his Chinese captors.

Examples of this can be seen on TV series like *The Bill*.

Unfair questioning can include physical or mental torture. The USA has been accused of unfair interrogation of terrorist suspects, due to their methods of interrogating prisoners for prolonged periods of time, without allowing them a break to sleep.

The future of human rights

A worldwide growth in human rights

Since 1948, when the Universal Declaration of Human Rights was signed, the idea of **human rights** has spread across the world. This growth has accelerated in the last ten years. The number of countries signing the six major human rights conventions and agreements has risen from 55 in 1990, to over 150 in 2000. Life expectancy has risen from a world average of 60 in 1975 to 65 in 2000. The number of countries with multi-party elections has risen from 28 in 1974 to 61 in 2000, meaning a much larger share of the world's population enjoy political rights.

Technology and human rights in the 21st century

Changes in technology mean a whole new set of threats to human rights now exist. With new technology, it is now possible to genetically clone plants and animals, monitor large areas of our cities using CCTV, and collect vast amounts of personal information on computer databases. This technology can be used to either help or hinder human rights.

In this context, human rights campaigners argue that the Universal Declaration of Human Rights looks out of date. The new European Charter of Fundamental Rights (see page 3) establishes new rights, limiting the effect technology has on our lives. These new rights include:

- **The right to respect the integrity of the human person**
  Everyone has the right to respect for their physical and mental integrity. This includes: a ban on the genetic screening of babies, a ban on financial gain from the human body and a ban on the reproductive cloning of human beings.

- **The right to data protection**
  This includes the right to determine for yourself whether any personal data may be disclosed and used.

- **The right to a private life**
  The right to respect for privacy, honour and reputation, home, and the confidentiality of correspondence and communications.

(see page 3)

Regional inequality

Despite this, there are large regional variations in human rights across the world. Five hundred million people, primarily in Africa and Asia, live in countries with a low level of development, depriving them of many basic social rights. One in four of the world's population lives in China, a one-party state which does not allow multi-party elections, and full freedom of speech. Poverty still exists in rich western democracies, such as the UK and the USA.

Discuss

Which human rights do you think should be a priority for governments to enforce? Give reasons for your views.

Does prostitution count as financial gain from the human body?

Discuss

Which of the new rights in the European Charter of Fundamental Rights do you think is the most important? Why?

'Smart' card could serve as passport and ID by 2006

Britons could be issued with 'smart' passports holding their fingerprints and other personal data within four years, the chief executive of the UK Passport Service said today.

Bernard Herdan said his plans for multipurpose passports would fit well with proposals from David Blunkett, the Home Secretary, for compulsory national identity cards. The 'biometric' cards, each with an ultra-slim microchip, could hold digital images of the holder's face, scans of the irises of their eyes and a full set of fingerprints.

Scanning stations could be set up at post offices or other designated centres, Mr Herdan said.

"This would allow us to link a person's identity to a biometric such as an iris scan, facial recognition, or a fingerprint. That would be a big step, but many countries are considering it."

Mr Blunkett announced earlier this month that he wanted to introduce so-called entitlement cards – his new phrase for compulsory national ID cards – that would carry details about state services each holder was entitled to, such as the NHS, social security and education.

The technology is already being used for asylum-seekers who have been issued with cards since 31 January 2002. Computer chips embedded in the cards carry details of each refugee's family members' nationality, date of birth, language and serial numbers.

ID cards – do we really need them?

Those in favour of ID cards, such as the Home Secretary, argue that there would be a range of benefits. Firstly, it would be easier to identify illegal immigrants, and terrorist suspects, thus improving everyone's right to security of person.

They would also enforce a person's right to an identity, by making fraud, such as credit card theft, more difficult. Finally, it would be easier for the government to identify false social security more easily.

Those against ID cards, such as the pressure group Liberty, argue that the threat to individual freedom outweighs the benefits of ID cards. They argue that ID cards would lead to an unacceptable lose of personal privacy.

After World War II, ID cards were quickly abolished, as many people complained of police harassment in times when they were stopped and asked for their papers. The Government points out that there are no current plans to introduce stop and search powers for the police. Liberty argues that once you introduce ID cards, they are open to misuse in the future.

Far left: CCTV cameras have become commonplace in both public and private areas as a security aid

Left: Footage from CCTV cameras is often monitored live, both to help prevent crime from occurring in the first place, and to catch the perpetrators when it occurs

Adapted from The Independent, 21 February 2001

Discuss

Read 'Smart card could serve as passport and ID by 2006'. Do you think ID cards are necessary to protect the right to security of UK citizens? Or do you consider them an infringement of human rights? Give reasons for your views.

Index and Glossary

Abortion
The act of terminating a pregnancy
(see pages 16–17).

Age of consent
The age at which it is legal to have sexual
intercourse (see page 21)

Amnesty International
An independent pressure group that
works to end human rights abuse
(see pages 2, 27).

Asylum
A form of protection that allows people to
stay in a foreign country for their own safety
(see pages 22–23).

Capital punishment
Punishment by death (see page 29).

Childcare
Looking after a child while the parents are at
work (see page 15).

Commission for Racial Equality (CRE)
The body responsible for enforcing the Race
Relations Act (see page 19).

Disability
The lack of the ability to do something
(see page 20).

Discrimination
Unfavourable treatment based on prejudice
against personal factors such as gender, race
or disability (see pages 2, 12, 14–15,
18–19, 20).

Emigrant
Someone who leaves a particular country to
live elsewhere (see page 22).

Entitlements
Things to which we have a fair claim or right
(see page 3).

Equal opportunities
Having the same right and opportunities as
anyone else to achieve a specific goal
(see pages 14–15).

Equal Opportunities Commission
A body set up to promote equal
opportunities in the UK (see page 14).

European Commission of Human Rights
The body responsible for investigating
human rights abuses in the European Union
(see page 3).

European Convention on Human Rights
A court of the European Union,
responsible for looking at cases in Europe
involving human rights abuses (see pages
2–3, 21, 29).

Euthanasia
Ending someone's life, usually with their
consent, to avoid prolonged suffering
(see page 25).

Free speech
The right to express opinions freely in public
(see page 24).

Full employment
When 95 per cent of the adult population
has a job (see page 12).

Human rights
The universal moral, legal and political
rights of the individual (see pages 1, 2–5,
11–12, 26–27, 28–29, 30).

Immigrant
Someone who arrives to live in a new
country (see pages 22–23).

Minimum wage
The lowest amount a person can legally be
paid (see pages 12–13).

Moral rights
The basic rights to fair, humane and equal
treatment (see page 1).

Persecution
Harassment or repeated violence, usually on
the grounds of race, politics or religion
(see pages 22–23).

Prejudice
Bias resulting from a preconceived opinion
(see page 18).

Pressure group
A group of people who seek to influence the
government, without actually taking power
themselves (see page 2).

Racism
Discrimination or prejudice on the grounds
of race (see page 18–19).

Refugee
Someone who has had to flee their country
against their wishes (see page 23).

Rights
The things to which everyone is morally or
legally entitled (see page 1).

Right to silence
The right of suspected criminals to remain
silent when under arrest (see page 28).

Torture
Physical abuse or mental pressure designed
to cause pain (see pages 2, 29).

Trade union
A group of workers who come together to
promote their common interests (see page 13).

UN Commission on Human Rights
The body responsible for monitoring human
rights abuses in UN countries (see pages 2, 6).

**United Nations Convention on the
Rights of the Child**
An agreement setting out the rights of children,
now part of international law (see pages 4, 16).

**United Nations High Commissioner
for Refugees (UNHCR)**
The head of a UN agency that helps refugees
around the world (see page 23).

**Universal Declaration of Human Rights
(UDHR)**
A UN document, signed in 1948, aimed at
safeguarding and protecting the human rights
of people around the world (see page 1).